DISASTERS AND THE ENVIRONMENT

TSUNAMIS
and the Environment

by Ailynn Collins

CAPSTONE PRESS
a capstone imprint

Published by Capstone Press, an imprint of Capstone
1710 Roe Crest Drive, North Mankato, Minnesota 56003
capstonepub.com

Copyright © 2025 by Capstone. All rights reserved. No part of this publication may be reproduced in whole or in part, or stored in a retrieval system, or transmitted in any form or by any means, electronic, mechanical, photocopying, recording, or otherwise, without written permission of the publisher.

Library of Congress Cataloging-in-Publication Data is available on the Library of Congress website.
ISBN: 9781669070894 (hardcover)
ISBN: 9781669070931 (paperback)
ISBN: 9781669070948 (ebook PDF)

Summary: Tsunamis can be more than 100 feet tall! After tsunamis crash into a coastline, their harmful effects can linger for years. Besides the impact to people, they can be disastrous for the environment. Tsunamis can strip sand from beaches and uproot trees. Salt from ocean water can seep into the ground and keep plants from growing. Tsunamis also kill many animals and destroy their homes. Learn about the important actions people are taking to help areas affected by tsunamis recover.

Editorial Credits
Editor: Carrie Sheely; Designer: Bobbie Nuytten; Media Researcher: Jo Miller; Production Specialist: Whitney Schaefer

Image Credits
Alamy: Design Pics Inc, 25, Hemis, 13, Robert Gilhooly, 26, Science History Images, 10, ZUMA Press, Inc., 27; AP Photo: Apichart Weerawong, 15; Getty Images: Lloyd Cluff, 11, Mark Meredith, 20, STR, 24; Shutterstock: Alexey UW, 16, Apiolff, cover (top), BlueRingMedia, 8, capture63, 9, Ethan Daniels, 17, Frans Delian, 7, Helissa Grundemann, 19, Michael Vi, 28, Paramarta Bari, 23, S.Narongrit99, cover (bottom), The Mariner 4291, 29; Superstock: Biosphoto/Sylvain Cordier, 21; U.S. Air Force photo by Master Sgt. Jeremy Lock, 5

Design Elements
Shutterstock: MAX79

Any additional websites and resources referenced in this book are not maintained, authorized, or sponsored by Capstone. All product and company names are trademarks™ or registered® trademarks of their respective holders.

TABLE OF CONTENTS

INTRODUCTION
Disaster in Japan................ 4

CHAPTER ONE
Ocean Waves.................. 6

CHAPTER TWO
Environmental Impacts.......... 10

CHAPTER THREE
Environment Recovery 14

CHAPTER FOUR
What Happens to Animals? 18

CHAPTER FIVE
Humans and Tsunamis.......... 24

Glossary 30
Read More 31
Internet Sites 31
Index..................... 32
About the Author 32

Words in **bold** are in the glossary.

Introduction

DISASTER IN JAPAN

On March 11, 2011, a powerful earthquake occurred in the Pacific Ocean about 80 miles (130 kilometers) from Japan. Thirty minutes later, a powerful tsunami slammed into Japan's Pacific coast. The largest wave was 131 feet (40 meters) tall.

The tsunami affected 1,242 miles (2,000 km) of Japan's coast. More than 18,000 people died in the natural disaster. More than 120,000 buildings were destroyed. Piles of **debris** were left behind.

FACT

A year after the 2011 Japan earthquake and tsunami, people walking along the beach in Oregon found a dock. It had floated across the Pacific Ocean from Misawa, Japan.

The tsunami also affected the **environment**. Farmlands as far as 3 miles (5 km) inland were flooded. Salt water, sand, and mud destroyed rice fields. Salt water had mixed in with the fresh water in the fields. This **brackish** water hurt crops. As a result, crops couldn't grow in these areas for a long time. Plants were killed along coastlines and beaches were destroyed.

The 2011 tsunami in Japan ripped apart buildings in its path, leaving rubble behind.

Chapter One

OCEAN WAVES

The word *tsunami* means "big wave" in Japanese. Most tsunami waves are less than 10 feet (3 m) high. These small waves don't usually cause widespread damage. But some tsunamis can be 100 feet (30 m) tall or more. These are the ones that cause the most damage.

How Do Tsunamis Happen?

What can cause tsunamis? Sometimes volcanic eruptions or landslides can create tsunamis. But earthquakes in the ocean are the most common cause. Earth's crust is made up of giant pieces of rock called tectonic plates. They lie under our oceans and continents.

The 2004 Indian Ocean earthquake and tsunami damaged the city of Banda Aceh, Indonesia.

Tectonic plates continually move. Sometimes they bump into each other and get stuck. Pressure builds. When the pressure becomes too much, the plates can suddenly move. The movement pushes the water up into a giant wave.

FACT
As tsunamis get near coasts, they slow down and get taller.

8

When a tsunami hits land, it can cause great destruction. People build cities, resorts, and homes on beaches and in coastal regions. These places can be easily destroyed by a tsunami. People and animals can be killed. The effects on the environment can be overlooked as people focus on the human impact.

Some scientists think climate change could cause more tsunamis around the world. Global warming can cause sea levels to rise as glaciers melt. Tsunamis then could more easily reach inland areas. Global warming can also lead to less stable soil, which can cause more landslides. Let's take a closer look at how nature can be affected by these powerful ocean waves.

In 2018, a tsunami damaged coastal areas of Indonesia.

Chapter Two

ENVIRONMENTAL IMPACTS

When a tsunami hits land, the water can strip away soil, sand, rocks, and plants. This is called **erosion**. Coastlines can be pushed farther inland. Erosion happens on the seafloor too. Plants, rocks, and sand get carried away. Animals that live there lose their homes and food sources.

Erosion can change the land and sea forever. For example, in 1958, a tsunami hit Lituya Bay in Alaska. Sections of land by the bay sank, while others rose higher. Plants and parts of forests were stripped away, and they never came back.

Land in Aceh, Indonesia, before and after the 2004 Indian Ocean tsunami

Case Study
1958 Lituya Bay Tsunami

The 1958 tsunami in Lituya Bay, Alaska, had the world's tallest recorded tsunami wave. It reached a height of up to 1,720 feet (524 m). Ninety million tons of rock slid into the water to cause the tsunami. The tsunami flattened thousands of trees and stripped away plants. It affected about 4 square miles (10 square kilometers) of land. Sixty years later, the scars of the damage can still be seen from space. Younger trees are growing along a new coastline that's much farther inland than it was before the tsunami.

Saltwater Problems

The flooding brought on by a tsunami can leave salt behind. Salt water from the ocean destroys plants. Many coastal plants cannot grow in water with a lot of salt. In 2004, a tsunami in the Indian Ocean destroyed an entire mangrove forest by the beaches in Phuket, Thailand. It also killed plants along the coast in the Maldives.

Groundwater collects under Earth's surface. It stays in the spaces between rocks and soil. Salt water from a tsunami can seep into the ground. Many crops and other plants then cannot absorb their much-needed **nutrients**. This means they won't grow properly. Farmland can take years to become usable again. When rice fields were destroyed by the 2011 tsunami in Japan, it took some farmland about three years before it was suitable for farm use again.

Mangrove trees were killed on Indonesia's Sumatra Island after the 2004 Indian Ocean tsunami.

13

Chapter Three

ENVIRONMENT RECOVERY

With time, the environment can recover. The time it takes depends on how an area was affected. People can help with the environment recovery process. They can clear away debris from human-made objects right away. They can also help restore natural environments such as mangrove forests. Mangrove trees are important to the protection of coastlines. Trees can be grown from seedlings. Scientists grow them in nurseries. People can then replant the trees in damaged areas that have been cleaned. Scientists can check that the water in which these trees will grow is once again brackish.

After the 2004 Indian Ocean tsunami, people planted mangrove and other trees in nurseries. The trees were then planted along Thailand's damaged coasts.

Coral Reefs

Coral reefs are important because they can protect coastlines from further tsunami damage. People can help regrow damaged coral reefs. Scientists can grow coral in labs and then replant them back into the ocean. They can remove plants that don't belong there to make room for new growth. People can even put in artificial reefs to replace parts that are beyond repair.

People sometimes grow coral on human-made metal structures.

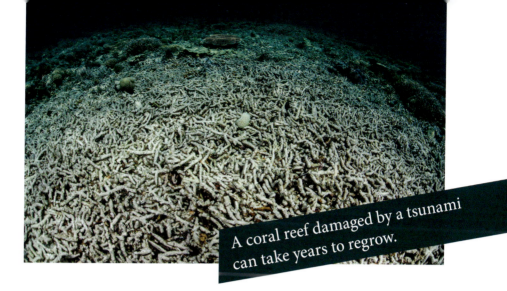

A coral reef damaged by a tsunami can take years to regrow.

Beaches

Scientists can monitor beaches after a tsunami to see how they recover. They take pictures of what the beach looked like before and after the tsunami. Some beaches may recover in several months. But researchers say that beaches can continue to change for several years after a tsunami.

Case Study
Seagrass Bed Recovery

In the 2004 Indian Ocean tsunami, the environment along the west coast of Thailand was affected. The Thai government conducted surveys. It was found that 3 to 10 percent of the seagrass beds were damaged. It took about six months for them to recover.

Chapter Four

WHAT HAPPENS TO ANIMALS?

In a tsunami, animals are greatly affected. Many land animals drown. Sea creatures can be tossed around and carried onto shore, where they die. Many insects can be killed by the force of the waves hitting them. These insects, along with uprooted plants, are food that other animals need. Without them, these animals may starve. Animals that survive can be lifted by giant waves. They may end up in a different environment that may not be suitable for living.

When a tsunami carries animals away from their homes, the creatures have to **adapt** to their new surroundings. Animals that are native to the area may now face different **predators** or have extra competition for food.

Dead fish along shorelines are a common sight after a tsunami.

Animal homes are also destroyed. Birds lose their nests when forests are stripped bare. Fish lose their places in seabeds and coral reefs. The homes of sea turtles are washed away as beaches are destroyed. For example, the 2004 Indian Ocean tsunami damaged nesting areas that leatherback sea turtles use on Andaman and Nicobar Islands. Sea urchins and abalone are picked up in the waves and dumped on land. These are food sources for other animals that may then go hungry.

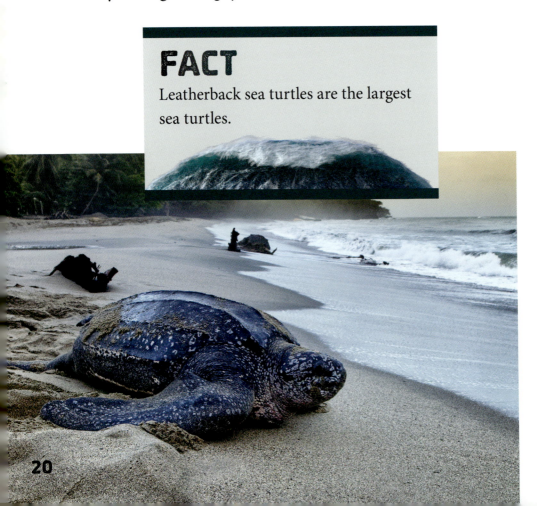

FACT
Leatherback sea turtles are the largest sea turtles.

The salt water that a tsunami brings can change freshwater areas such as lakes, ponds, and rivers. Animals that need fresh water end up with brackish water. Animals such as trout, bass, frogs, salamanders, and crayfish are likely to die in this environment. Land animals that rely on this water to drink also suffer when water turns brackish.

Laysan albatross care for their young after a tsunami that hit Hawaii.

Tsunamis break pipelines and damage ships. Oil, sewage, and other poisons enter the environment. Dangerous chemicals may enter the ocean, poisoning marine life. Waves can carry these pollutants to fresh water on land. The water can then be dangerous for land animals to drink.

Animal Super Senses

After the 2004 Indian Ocean tsunami, rescuers in Sri Lanka noticed that fewer animal carcasses than expected were found on the beaches. They wondered if the animals had known that something dangerous was coming. Later, people reported that elephants in the area had screamed and run inland before the tsunami. Flamingos had also left their nesting areas in a hurry. Bats had flown away from their caves just before the tsunami hit. Experts believed that the animals' senses of hearing and smell helped them know that a tsunami was on its way.

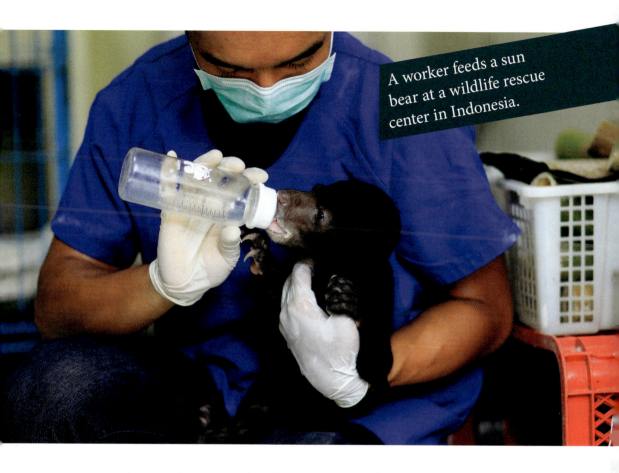
A worker feeds a sun bear at a wildlife rescue center in Indonesia.

How Animals Recover

Wildlife can recover from a tsunami over time. They may recover more quickly if they have help. People can rescue stranded animals. After taking care of injuries and illness the animals may have, people can return them to their natural homes. If those homes are destroyed, animals may be rehomed in protected wildlife parks. People can also help remove animals that don't belong in an area to help the **habitat** recover.

Chapter Five

HUMANS AND TSUNAMIS

Tsunamis also impact the lives of humans. Entire towns can flood. Buildings can be destroyed, and roads can rip open. The 2004 Indian Ocean tsunami hit the coasts of 17 nearby countries. It killed about 200,000 people and caused billions of dollars in property damage.

Wreckage floats near Marina Beach in India after the 2004 tsunami hit the area.

After a tsunami, bacteria and other pollutants can get into drinking water supplies. People using this water can become sick or die. After the 2004 Indian Ocean tsunami, drinking water supplies were affected in the Maldives. The United Nations Children's Fund (UNICEF) helped provide desalination units to people. These units change salt water into fresh water so that people can safely drink the water.

When crops are destroyed, farmers can lose their source of income. Stores that buy their crops lose products to sell. People can suffer from a limited food supply.

Members of the Australian armed forces provided clean drinking water to people affected by the Indian Ocean tsunami.

Rebuilding

The most immediate job after a tsunami is to rescue stranded and trapped people. Organizations and volunteers help get people to safety using boats and helicopters. They provide temporary shelter, food, and medical care for those who need it.

Once people are rescued and safe, the damaged areas need to be cleaned up. It's important to move debris away carefully so that no one is hurt. Sometimes people burn debris. But burning some items can cause pollution. Experts are needed to guide the cleanup efforts to keep people and the environment safe.

Finally, homes, businesses, and roads need to be rebuilt. This takes time. Some scientists studying countries that suffer from many tsunamis think that rebuilding takes between five and 10 years.

Cleanup efforts after a tsunami can require diggers and other large machines.

Case Study
2011 Nuclear Disaster

In March 2011, the tsunami in Japan damaged four reactors at a **nuclear** power plant in Fukushima. Scientists were afraid that the **radiation** released into the environment could cause cancer or other diseases.

Nearly 10 years later, a report said that Fukushima residents had no reported health effects. But some people in the area do remain concerned. The cleanup there may take up to 40 years.

Preparing for Future Disasters

There will always be tsunamis, so it is important to be prepared. Is there a way to know when a tsunami is coming? In 1948, two years after a disastrous tsunami hit Hawaii, scientists in the United States created the Pacific Tsunami Warning System. Over the years, they've improved it. In 1952, Japan created its warning system.

Today, scientists are still not able to predict exactly when and where a tsunami will strike. But tools are helping them learn more. Sensors on the seafloor can send information about earthquakes to computers. These can tell scientists which earthquakes might cause a tsunami.

Tsunamis are deadly disasters. They have big impacts on people, animals, and the environment. As we learn more about them and how to be prepared, we can lessen the damage they do.

A tsunami detection buoy floats in the Indian Ocean.

Glossary

adapt (uh-DAPT)—to change to fit into a new or different environment

brackish (BRA-kish)—somewhat salty

debris (duh-BREE)—the scattered pieces of something that has been broken or destroyed

environment (in-VY-ruhn-muhnt)—the natural world of the land, water, and air

erosion (i-ROH-zhuhn)—wearing away of rock or soil by wind, water, or ice

habitat (HAB-i-tat)—the natural place and conditions in which a plant or animal lives

nuclear (NOO-klee-ur)—having to do with the energy created by splitting atoms; nuclear reactors use this energy as a power source

nutrient (NOO-tree-ent)—a substance needed by a living thing to stay healthy

predator (PRED-uh-tur)—an animal that hunts other animals for food

radiation (ray-dee-AY-shuhn)—tiny particles sent out from radioactive material

Read More

Burgan, Michael. *Fighting to Survive Natural Disasters: Terrifying True Stories*. North Mankato, MN: Capstone, 2020.

Romero, Libby. *Built to Survive Natural Disasters*. New York: DK Publishing, 2023.

Williams, Olivia. *Understanding Earthquakes and Tsunamis*. Ann Arbor, MI: Cherry Lake Press, 2022.

Internet Sites

NASA Space Place: What Is a Tsunami?
spaceplace.nasa.gov/tsunami/en

National Geographic Kids: Tsunami Facts: Check Out the Mighty Wave!
natgeokids.com/uk/discover/geography/physical-geography/tsunamis

SMS Tsunami Warning: Tsunamis: The Effects
sms-tsunami-warning.com/pages/tsunami-effects

Index

animals, 9, 10, 18, 19, 20, 21, 22, 23, 29
animal senses, 22

beaches, 4, 5, 9, 12, 17, 20, 22, 24

corals, 16, 17, 20
crops, 5, 12, 25

drinking water, 25

earthquakes, 4, 6, 7, 29
erosion, 10

glaciers, 9
global warming, 9

Indian Ocean tsunami, 7, 12, 13, 15, 17, 20, 22, 24, 25, 29

Indonesia, 7, 9, 13, 23

landslides, 6, 9
Lituya Bay, 10, 11

mangrove forests, 12, 14

nuclear power plants, 27
nurseries, 14, 15

Pacific Tsunami Warning System, 28
pollution, 22, 25, 26

replanting, 14, 16

tectonic plates, 6, 8
Thailand, 12, 15, 17

About the Author

Ailynn Collins has written many books for children. They include stories about aliens and monsters to books about science, space, and the future. These are her favorite subjects. She lives outside Seattle with her family and six dogs. When she's not writing, she enjoys participating in dog shows and dog sports.